One-Pot *paleo*

SIMPLE TO MAKE, DELICIOUS TO EAT *and* GLUTEN-FREE TO BOOT

Jenny Castaneda

founder of Paleo Foodie Kitchen

PAGE STREET
PUBLISHING CO.

PAGE STREET
PUBLISHING CO.

First published in 2015 by
Page Street Publishing Co.
27 Congress Street, Suite 103
Salem, MA 01970
www.pagestreetpublishing.com

Distributed by Macmillan; sales in Canada by The Canadian Manda Group; distribution in Canada by The Jaguar Book Group.

18   17   16   15   1   2   3   4   5

ISBN-13: 978-1-62414-122-5
ISBN-10: 1-62414-122-6

Library of Congress Control Number: 2014950224

Cover and book design by Page Street Publishing Co.
Photography by Jenny Castaneda

Printed and bound in China

Page Street is proud to be a member of 1% for the Planet. Members donate one percent of their sales to one or more of the over 1,500 environmental and sustainability charities across the globe who participate in this program.

To my mom, Marly. This one's for you.

CONTENTS

Sizzling Cast Iron

Comforting Casseroles

Scrumptious Stir-Fries

Bake, Broil or Grill

Warming Soups and Stews

Sensational Salads

The Basics

Foreword

From the moment Jenny told us she was writing *One-Pot Paleo* we were impressed and excited about the concept! After running our own website and writing several bestselling cookbooks, we know first-hand how much people struggle to make this lifestyle work for them in the long haul. Navigating those difficulties and figuring out how to make it work in real life is how Paleo becomes a lifestyle, instead of just a diet. Having a resource to help us make Paleo easier provides a life line for so many busy people—and *One-Pot Paleo* does just that!

It won't be a surprise to anyone that one of the hardest parts of going Paleo is moving away from simple, pre-made foods toward making everything from scratch. But using the method of cooking entire meals in one pot simplifies something that can be overwhelming to many. Not only does it save time and effort when cooking, but having a meal on the table without a huge mess in the kitchen is an amazing accomplishment!

All of that does you no good, however, if the food isn't satisfying once made. I'm here to tell you, that is not a concern with the recipes you'll find in the pages to follow. We knew we'd like the recipes from having followed Jenny and her blog, Paleo Foodie Kitchen, on social media for years. What we didn't anticipate, however, is how well the book would come together and be packed with gorgeous, drool-worthy, inventive, bold, flavorful, colorful, rich, deliciousness!

When the family sat down and paged through the recipes in *One-Pot Paleo* we couldn't narrow down which we wanted to try to a list of even less than a dozen. With a seemingly genius approach to international cuisine, we're thrilled to try out the Japanese Hot Pot, the Japchae Noodles and the Peruvian Chicken Lime Soup. Our favorites ranged from nut-free, dairy-free Plantain Pizza to the incredible Dutch Baby and the Hawaiian Meatballs. And how could we go wrong with Aromatic Mussels or Fifteen-Minute Ginger Chicken Noodles?

Furthermore, we love Jenny's progressive approach to defining Paleo. Unlike the rigid rules of yesteryear, Paleo is now viewed as a template for each of us to tailor to our own body's ever changing needs. For some of us that means absolutely no grains but inclusion of high-quality dairy, for others, safe starches like white rice help us regulate hormones and maintain health without derailing gut health. In *One-Pot Paleo* you'll find nourishing, healing true superfoods like broth, organ meats, vegetables and seafood as well as recipes using rice and butter to expand your Paleo template. And the Allergen Index will allow anyone with food sensitivities (like our family) to find recipes that work for their particular needs.

We found comfort and joy in reading Jenny's recipes. The photos are spectacular and with each page we found ourselves more and more impressed with what was able to be accomplished in one dish. Don't be afraid to sit down and curl up with a mug of something warm (perhaps the Chicken Broth) to read the whole book cover to cover—we recommend you grab a big pile of sticky notes first; you'll wanna flag all the recipes to try later!

—**Stacy Toth and Matthew McCarry**, authors of *Real Life Paleo*, *Beyond Bacon*, *Eat Like a Dinosaur* and bloggers at the popular website PaleoParents.com

Introduction

All of my fondest memories growing up involved food, from weekly Sunday lunches after church to the 12 dishes my family cooked in a day to ring in each New Year. On Saturday mornings at 11:00 a.m., my mom and I would tune in to our favorite cooking shows on TV. She always had her pencil and notepad ready to jot down recipes that looked good and were worth trying. I particularly liked those that were easy to make so I wouldn't have to wait too long to eat!

Living in a traditional Filipino household, we had our usual fare that could be deemed unhealthy because it involved a lot of frying, packed seasonings and mixes with MSG. What a lot of people don't know, though, is that there's a wide variety of Filipino food involving vegetables and protein that are fairly nutritious. Yes, I did eat junk food and sweets, but my mom always made sure that I ate a balanced diet to make up for those times that I ate poorly.

After I got married, my eating habits took a nosedive. Most of our meals came from a box in the form of Hamburger Helper and macaroni and cheese. We ate out a lot, and fast food was part of our weekly rotation. Tired of feeling sluggish all the time, I started calorie counting and restricted myself to 1,200 calories a day in order to shed the excess pounds I had gained. I ate low-fat foods and did basic cardio exercises 3 times a week, and within 6 months I was at a healthy weight and had dropped 3 dress sizes. I'd found something that finally worked for me, and eating healthy became my new obsession.

My low-fat, calorie-counting diet had been consistent for years when in 2011 I was first introduced to Paleo. My kettlebell teacher, Junior, at NDS Athletics handed out reading materials about this eating lifestyle after class one day. I read it twice and didn't think that I could give up a lot of things I am used to eating, so I put it away. After all, I was able to maintain my weight by keeping my calorie intake in check, and the thought of eating more fat instead of carbohydrates turned me off.

A year later, while I was doing some online research on how I could live a healthier lifestyle and eat more whole foods and less processed products, I crossed paths with Paleo once again. I spent countless hours reading sites, blogs and forums, overloading my mind with all the information I could find. It was then that I finally decided to give it a shot. I had nothing to lose, and if it didn't work for me, at least I knew I was eating in a way that was good for my body.

Honestly, it was a gradual introduction that took months of trial and error. My husband was still eating fast food, chips and gluten-based products, so trying to eat Paleo amidst the food temptations in the house was my biggest challenge. Instead of forcing him to embrace Paleo, I figured I would lead by example and cook exciting dishes that were colorful, filled with flavor and totally satisfying. After a while, meal planning became easier and making the right choices became a no-brainer. This has become a way of life. I eat close to 85 percent Paleo and my husband is at 70 percent and I couldn't be any happier!

I went through a few rounds of eating strictly Paleo and felt the positive effects of eliminating processed food, gluten, dairy, sugar, legumes and alcohol. I slept better and deeper, averaging 6 to 7 hours each night, so I had consistent energy throughout the day. All the things that I thought were normal became better:

the bloating disappeared, the migraines got better and the cravings lessened. I also had more stamina for agility drills, tabata and intense conditioning at kettlebell class. I progressed to a heavier set of weights and felt stronger swinging a 48.5 pound (22 kg) bell. For my petite 5 foot (152-cm) and 112 pound (51-kg) frame, this was definitely a big achievement.

After reading books and educating myself further, I came up with my own modified approach that incorporates occasional white rice, grass-fed butter and safe starches such as arrowroot and tapioca. My body tolerates these pretty well. I found that rice, especially, gave me more endurance and energy when I worked out. I also gave myself some leverage to enjoy life by partaking in a gluten-free treat or two and making the best choices based on what is available at family gatherings and special occasions so I don't feel left out and deprived. I do not strive for Paleo perfection, and this is the protocol that works for me. I always advise people to experiment and find their own protocol, since Paleo clearly isn't a one-size-fits-all lifestyle.

From my pre–Paleo days until now, I view good food as one of the simple pleasures in my life. To me, it is the center of great conversations, it brings family and friends together and it is a firsthand experience in learning about a culture.

I hope the recipes in this book will be an inspiration and a good resource not just for those interested or starting out on Paleo, but also for those currently living this lifestyle. May each recipe serve as an invitation to enjoy more home-cooked meals while gathered around the dinner table with family and friends.

From my kitchen to yours, happy cooking!

jenny aratomich

"You don't have to cook fancy or complicated masterpieces —just good food from fresh ingredients."

—JULIA CHILD

What Is One-Pot Paleo?

Sometimes even the simplest recipe calls for multiple pans—a cast-iron pan to cook and sear meat, plus a skillet to sauté sides and a saucepot to create a reduction. Three extra pans are now piled on your sink next to the tower of dishes that are already begging to be washed.

Imagine preparing a meal without having to figure out which sides to pair with what entrée. A complete meal consisting of protein, vegetables and the right amount of carbohydrates with just one cooking pan to clean up! It's certainly a win-win situation.

This book does not focus on just one type of cooking vessel, rather it expands to those that each household regularly uses such as a cast-iron pan, wok, skillet, casserole/baking dish, stockpot, Dutch oven pan, braiser, baking sheet and even a charcoal or gas grill. Using any or even all of these opens a whole world of possibilities in terms of one-pot cooking. Of course if you do not possess the one mentioned in a recipe, get creative and substitute what you have available. No wok—how about a skillet? No braiser—a Dutch oven pan will do. No casserole—a cast-iron pan or skillet work as well. You get the drift. Use your best judgment and don't go out and buy additional pots and pans unless you absolutely need to.

From what I've read and heard, one of the biggest misconceptions about one-pot cooking is it can taste bland and boring because ingredients are generally tossed into a pan and set on a stove to cook. You definitely wont find that here! Each recipe is packed with flavor that I can guarantee will be well received by the palate.

As you skim through the recipes in this book, you'll find some that are quick and easy and come together in less than an hour, which are perfect for weeknights. Those that are simmered or braised for hours to achieve maximum flavor are ideal for weekends, and those that are marinated overnight can be prepared the night before, therefore transitioning into a quick-and-easy meal the next day.

Another goal I had for this book was to make use of ingredients that are commonly found in regular grocery and health food stores so you wouldn't have to hunt down that one special ingredient just to make a dish. The spices and seasonings used are those that you probably have in your spice cabinet already; if not, they are easily accessible. Even my Chicken Biryani (page 70) recipe with the most spices has been toned down without sacrificing flavor.

If all of this sounds good to you, then find a chapter to cook from, pick a recipe and start cooking!

The Story Behind the Recipes in This Book

I've always looked at food not just as a way to nourish the body, but also as something that delights the senses and comforts the soul. Behind each dish is a story, a meaning and a way of life.

A large part of my cooking style is influenced by my Filipino heritage and Spanish ancestry. Filipino food can be characterized as a melting pot of flavors reflecting 333 years of colonization by Spain back in the 1500s, as well as adaptations of American, Chinese and other Asian cuisines. Aside from the usual *adobo*, *pancit* and *lumpia* that almost everyone knows about, there are a lot of other delicious dishes that have never gone mainstream.

I wanted to showcase the healthier side of Filipino food so I created Paleo versions of the dishes that I grew up eating. Surprising to some, I only had to make minor tweaks since many ingredients are already Paleo compliant. Of course there are a few that needed a total overhaul such as the Filipino Chicken BBQ (page 112), but I'm proud of the end result because it still tastes pretty close to the real thing!

There are also recipes that were travel inspired. My husband and I are avid travelers, and we make it a point to visit 1 to 2 new countries each year. We forgo the overpriced touristy restaurants for hole-in-the-wall joints and even food carts along the street so we can get firsthand experience of what the locals like to eat. It's also a good way to learn and understand a new culture, which contributes to a deeper appreciation for its food. While we've really enjoyed a ton of dishes, not all of our favorites are in this book. I focused on dishes that we've eaten multiple times on each trip, like the Irish Stew (page 153) and Moorish Skewers (page 127).

The remaining majority of the recipes are a combination of dishes from our favorite places to eat as well as quick-and-easy meals that I prepare at home on a regular basis. When eating out, I have a habit of dissecting my meal and taking mental notes on how I can recreate it using a few substitutions. I remember a time when I even quizzed our server on my entrée's exact ingredients!

I also added a section that lists the basics used in recipes throughout this book. From 3 different types of broth (make them all and you'll never run out!), to sauces and my tried-and-true method for cooking white rice, because being Filipino I've mastered this technique from childhood.

Each recipe in this book is unique and will take your senses on a journey as you cook one-pot Paleo!

Ingredient Swaps and Substitutions

Below is a table you can use as a guide if a specific recipe calls for an ingredient that is not strictly Paleo. These are used in small amounts throughout the book and don't pose an issue with most individuals, but if you have a major intolerance to any of these ingredients, use the appropriate alternative or omit it from the recipe.

INGREDIENT	ALTERNATIVE
White Rice	Cauliflower Rice
Butter	Ghee or Coconut Oil
Red/White Wine	Chicken/Beef Bone Broth
Worcestershire	Coconut Aminos
Arrowroot	Omit
Tapioca Flour	Omit

chapter one

SIZZLING CAST IRON

The wonderfully delicious sound coming from a sizzling cast-iron pan will be enough to make your tummy grumble and your mouth water. A delectable aroma teases your senses, giving you an idea of what's to come. In a short amount of time, good food will make its way to the table, and you will be able to immediately dive in and feast while it's still piping hot.

I almost always reach for my cast-iron pan when I am preparing meals at home. It can cook up almost any meal (well, except soup). From my Salmon Scramble (page 46), to Pan-Seared Steak with Caramelized Shallots (page 14) and Mushroom Meat Pizza (page 25)—this versatile pan can handle it all.

The recipes in this section are one-pot meals that you can make using a cast-iron pan. Some can be cooked together and some are cooked in batches, where the protein is cooked first followed by the vegetables. I've even thrown in 2 sweet pancake recipes (page 41 and 42) that are perfect for breakfast or as a dessert to share!

Pan-Seared Steak
with Caramelized Shallots

SERVES
2

On my blog I have a go-to steak recipe that is part of our dinner rotation because it's so easy to make and steak for dinner always makes my husband happy. Who doesn't love steak anyway?! This is a different variation that uses a combination of fragrant rosemary and thyme. It adds an earthy and aromatic flavor to the butter and caramelized shallots as it reduces into a rich and decadent sauce, turning a good cut of steak into something amazing. The addition of sautéed asparagus spears rounds this up to a simple yet gourmet meal!

2 (10 oz [300 g]) rib eye steaks, 1″ (2.5 cm) thick

½ tsp coarse salt, I prefer Himalayan

½ tsp cracked black pepper

2 tbsp (30 ml) ghee or tallow

1 tbsp (15 g) salted butter

1 c (160 g) shallots, sliced

1 tsp dried rosemary, crushed

½ tsp dried thyme, crushed

½ lb (225 g) fresh asparagus spears, woody ends trimmed off

¼ c (60 ml) Beef Bone Broth (page 185)

Bring the steaks to room temperature at least 30 minutes before cooking so they won't be cold in the middle and overcooked on the outside. Season the steaks with coarse salt and black pepper on both sides.

Heat a cast-iron pan over high heat. Once the pan starts smoking, add 2 tablespoons (30 ml) of ghee and place the steaks on the pan. Cook 4 minutes on the first side for medium rare. Flip to the other side and cook for another 4 minutes. Remove cooked steaks from the pan and place them on a plate. Cover with foil to rest.

Reduce the pan's heat to medium. Add the butter, shallots, rosemary and thyme. Cook for 5 minutes until the shallots begin to caramelize. Add the asparagus and sauté for 2 minutes. Add the Beef Bone Broth and simmer for 5 minutes until the asparagus is cooked. Scoop the shallots and pan drippings over the cooked steaks and serve the asparagus on the side.

Skirt Steak Fajitas

SERVES
4

I order fajitas all the time when I eat out because they're Paleo compliant. When I make this dish at home, I forgo the premade seasonings with unhealthy additives and opt for fresh ingredients to make a simple marinade. Ordinary skirt steak comes out tender with a warm, citrusy flavor and a little bit of a kick thanks to some cumin, chili, cilantro and lime. You'll know you're in for a special treat because your entire house will smell so good while the meat is searing on the hot cast-iron pan. Triple the amount of vegetables and you won't even miss the tortillas or beans!

MARINADE

6 cloves garlic, minced

¼ c (60 ml) extra virgin olive oil

¼ c (60 ml) coconut aminos

1 ½ tsp (5 g) cumin

1 tsp chili powder

¼ c (10 g) cilantro, chopped

Juice and zest of 2 limes

1 ½ lb (675 g) skirt steak

Sea salt

Black pepper

1 red bell pepper, sliced into strips

1 yellow bell pepper, sliced into strips

1 green bell pepper, sliced into strips

1 large onion, sliced into strips

2 jalapeños, stem and seeds removed, sliced into strips

2 avocados, sliced

1 beefsteak tomato, chopped

¼ c (10 g) cilantro, chopped

Combine all the marinade ingredients in a gallon-sized (3 ¾ L) zip-top plastic bag. Place the skirt steak in the bag, press out the excess air and seal. Lightly massage the bag to make sure the marinade coats every inch of the skirt steak. Place it in the fridge to marinate for 1 hour.

Heat a cast-iron pan over medium-high heat. Remove the skirt steak from the bag and set aside the remaining liquid. Generously season both sides of the skirt steak with sea salt and black pepper. Place the steak on the pan and sear for 5 minutes. Flip to the other side for another 5 minutes for medium. Remove from the pan. Place it on a cutting board and cover with foil to rest.

While the skirt is resting, scrape off any excess burned brown bits that are stuck to the bottom of the pan. Add the sliced bell peppers, onion and jalapeños. Add the marinade that was used for the meat and sauté vegetables for 4 to 5 minutes. Turn off the heat. Thinly slice the skirt steak across the grain and place it on a large serving plate. Top with the cooked fajita vegetables, avocado slices, chopped tomato and cilantro.

Portobello Sandwich

SERVES
4

Who says sandwiches should only be made with bread? Not me! Eating Paleo means thinking outside the box most of the time, and I love using meaty portobellos instead of bread for sandwiches. They are extremely versatile and can hold up to high heat without falling apart. Plus, don't they look super cool? For a small fee, some burger places will gladly grill them up as a substitute for bread buns. Try this sandwich with sautéed vegetables and prosciutto slices for a portable snack or filling lunch on the go.

8 large portobello mushrooms

6 tsp (30 ml) bacon fat

1 large onion, thinly sliced

1 ½ c (85 g) sun-dried tomatoes, cut into strips

2 bunches spinach

Black pepper

4 tsp (20 ml) whole grain Dijon mustard

4 strips prosciutto

Clean the portobello mushroom caps by gently wiping with a damp paper towel. Using a small spoon, scrape off the gills from each cap and remove the stem in the middle.

Add 2 teaspoons (10 ml) of bacon fat to a cast-iron pan over medium heat. Add the onions and sun-dried tomatoes. Sauté for 5 minutes until the onions are soft. Add the spinach and sauté until wilted, about 1 to 2 minutes. Season with black pepper and set aside.

Lightly oil the top and bottom of the portobello mushrooms with the remaining 4 teaspoons (20 ml) of bacon fat. Due to their size, cook the mushrooms two at a time. Place the mushrooms cap side down on the same pan over medium-high heat. Cook for 3 minutes, flip and cook the other side for another 3 minutes. Remove and set aside.

To assemble each sandwich, take a cooked portobello mushroom cap side down and spread 1 teaspoon of mustard. Add the sautéed vegetables, a strip of prosciutto and top with another mushroom, cap side up.

Cut in half before serving.

Loaded Spanish Tortilla

SERVES
6

My husband and I first had this dish, fondly called *Tortilla de Patata*, at a tapas bar in Seville located in the Andalusian region of Spain. Paired with aromatic slices of *jamón ibérico de belotta* and a strong cup of coffee, this dish was something we looked forward to each morning. I enhanced the original version with prosciutto and sun-dried tomatoes for an added flavor dimension and to make it a complete meal while preserving its authenticity. Preparing it is a little bit involved and requires an extra bowl to hold batches of cooked potatoes and whisk the eggs, but it is worth it. This tortilla will take your taste buds on a culinary adventure to Seville!

¼ c (60 ml) ghee or tallow

½ c (65 g) onion, thinly sliced

1 c (55 g) sun-dried tomatoes, chopped

1 ½ lb (675 g) potatoes, thinly sliced

12 large eggs, room temperature

½ tsp sea salt

¼ tsp black pepper

6 slices prosciutto

In a cast-iron pan over medium heat, melt 1 tablespoon (15 ml) of ghee. Add the onions and sun-dried tomatoes. Sauté for 6 minutes until the onions are soft and translucent. Remove from the pan and set aside in a bowl.

Fry the potatoes in 3 batches using 1 tablespoon (15 ml) of ghee for each one. Cook each batch for 5 minutes and set aside. Turn off the heat. Move the cooked onions and potatoes to the pan. Crack and whisk the eggs in the same bowl used to store the onions and potatoes. Season with sea salt and black pepper. Add the potatoes, onions and sun-dried tomatoes to the whisked eggs and gently mix everything together. Pour this mixture back into the pan and reduce the heat to low. Cover and cook for 6 to 7 minutes or until eggs are firm and set on top.

Turn the broiler on high. Add the prosciutto slices on top of the tortilla and broil for 5 minutes to crisp up the prosciutto. Remove the pan from the broiler and cool for a few minutes before slicing and serving.

note: Use a mandolin to quickly and evenly slice the onion and potatoes.

Dutch Baby

**SERVES
2**

It took me multiple tries and more than a dozen eggs while channeling my inner baking goddess before I nailed the right liquid-starch combination to get this Dutch Baby to produce some height. Though it doesn't overflow from the pan like its gluten-based version, this comes out light and puffy, crispy on the outside and custardy on the inside just the way it should be!

3 large eggs, room temperature

¾ c (180 ml) Coconut Milk (page 187)

¼ tsp vanilla extract

3 tbsp (20 g) coconut flour, sifted

½ c (60 g) tapioca flour

¼ tsp cinnamon powder

½ tsp baking powder

3 tbsp (45 g) butter, unsalted

2 tbsp (25 g) coconut sugar

½ lb (225 g) strawberries, tops removed and quartered

Juice and zest of 1 lemon

Place a cast-iron pan inside the oven and preheat it to 425°F (220°C).

Crack the eggs in a large bowl. Using a handheld mixer or immersion blender whisk them for 15 to 20 seconds. Add the coconut milk and vanilla extract. Blend for 10 seconds. Add the coconut flour, tapioca flour, cinnamon powder and baking powder. Blend continuously until the lumps are gone. Scrape down the sides when needed. Let it rest for 5 minutes to give the coconut flour time to absorb enough liquid.

Add the butter to the pan and return it to the oven for 3 minutes until the butter melts and becomes frothy. Pour the batter into the center of the pan and place it in the oven to cook for 30 minutes. It is ready once it has puffed up with a golden brown color.

To make powdered coconut sugar, place the coconut sugar crystals in a coffee grinder and pulse until it is pulverized.

Combine the strawberries, lemon juice and zest and spread it on top of the Dutch Baby. Top with powdered coconut sugar and serve immediately.

Seared Scallops with Pancetta and Brussels Sprouts

SERVES
2

A plate of seared scallops set atop a bed of seasoned sprouts is a fancy-looking meal that doesn't take much effort and is sure to please. You've got something good going on when you see that beautiful golden brown crust develop on each flaky scallop! It is the crowning glory that enhances the delicate flavor of the scallops without overpowering them. As a finishing touch, fresh lemon juice and zest perk up the entire dish and tie everything together. Shredding the sprouts will add a few minutes to your prep time, but it will cut the cooking time in half because doing so makes them soften easily after a quick stir-fry.

¼ c (60 ml) ghee

4 oz (115 g) pancetta, chopped

1 lb (450 g) Brussels sprouts, shredded

¼ c (60 ml) water

Zest of 1 lemon

1 lb (450 g) large scallops, rinsed and dried thoroughly with a paper towel

⅛ tsp paprika

¼ tsp sea salt

¼ tsp black pepper

Juice of 1 lemon

Add 1 tablespoon (15 ml) of ghee to a cast-iron pan over medium-high heat. Add the pancetta and sauté until it starts to turn crispy, about 2 minutes. Reduce the heat to medium. Add the shredded Brussels sprouts, mix, cover and cook for 5 to 8 minutes. Add water to deglaze and scrape off the brown bits from the bottom of the pan. Season with lemon zest. Remove from the pan and set aside on a serving plate.

Season one side of the scallops with paprika, sea salt and black pepper. In the same pan used for the Brussels sprouts, melt the remaining 3 tablespoons (45 ml) of ghee. Cook the scallops in 2 batches to avoid overcrowding them. Once the pan is hot, add the scallops seasoned side down and sear for 3 minutes until they develop a brown crust. Flip to the other side and sear for another 3 minutes. Remove from the pan and arrange on top of the shredded Brussels sprouts.

Drizzle with lemon juice before serving.

Calamari with Marinara

SERVES 2

One day when I was in San Francisco for work, I was lucky enough to nab a seat during happy hour at a seafood restaurant in the Ferry Building. On the menu was a seasonal calamari dish that I ordered with a dozen half-priced oysters. The chef made my order in 5 minutes tops, and in no time I was scarfing down a smoking hot plate of super-fresh calamari. I've had that dish in the back of my mind ever since, so when I finally had the chance, I gave it a whirl. I tossed sliced squid with marinara sauce and served it with wilted chard finished off with a squeeze of fresh lemon juice. Voila! It tastes exactly the way I remember it—perfectly cooked calamari with a garlicky tomato sauce. This complete seafood meal can be ready in less than 10 minutes!

1 lb (450 g) squid, cleaned and cut into ½" (1.5 cm) rings

1 tbsp (15 ml) ghee or coconut oil

2 cloves garlic, minced

1 c (225 ml) Marinara Sauce (page 189)

1 bunch Swiss chard, torn into bite-sized pieces

Sea salt

Black pepper

1 lemon, cut into wedges

Blot and dry the squid pieces using a paper towel to remove excess water.

Heat a cast-iron pan over high heat and melt the ghee. Add the squid and garlic. Sauté for 1 minute.

Reduce the heat to medium and add the marinara sauce and Swiss chard. Season with sea salt and black pepper. Sauté for 2 more minutes until the squid is opaque and cooked through. Turn off the heat and season with freshly squeezed lemon before serving.

Lemon Butter Swordfish

SERVES
2

Swordfish has a firm and meaty texture that can withstand frying without falling apart. I like to make it when we're craving something other than steak or I see wild swordfish on sale. I jazz it up a little bit with a light aromatic marinade that accentuates its mild flavor. Creamy butter and the bright zest of lemons create a luscious sauce that is pleasantly light. Remember not to cook each side longer than necessary. You don't want to end up with rubbery swordfish for dinner!

Juice and zest of 1 lemon

2 cloves garlic, minced

1 tbsp (15 ml) extra virgin olive oil

2 tbsp (30 ml) coconut aminos

¼ tsp sea salt

¼ tsp black pepper

⅛ tsp red pepper flakes

2 (8 oz [225 g]) swordfish steaks

2 tbsp (30 ml) ghee or coconut oil

½ lb (225 g) fresh asparagus spears, woody ends trimmed off

3 tbsp (45 g) unsalted butter

Combine the juice of half a lemon, garlic, extra virgin olive oil, coconut aminos, sea salt, black pepper and red pepper flakes. Pour over the swordfish steaks and marinate for 1 hour.

Add ghee to a cast-iron pan over medium-high heat. Add the swordfish and set aside the excess marinade. Sear each side for 3 minutes. Remove from the pan and set aside.

Scrape off any browned bits that may be stuck to the bottom of the pan. Add the asparagus to the same pan and fry for 3 minutes. Sauté until they turn dark green.

Move the asparagus to one side and return the swordfish to the pan. Lower the heat to medium-low and add the marinade used for the fish, unsalted butter, lemon zest and juice of the remaining lemon half. Swirl it around, scoop up the seasoned melted butter and drizzle it on top of the asparagus and swordfish. Simmer for 3 minutes to let the flavors meld together. Remove from the heat and serve.

Stuffed Squid

SERVES
4

Squid is a mild-tasting seafood that can be filled with any type of meat or vegetable, making it a Paleo-friendly alternative to breaded calamari. Cleaning fresh squid is really easy to do at home, or if you prefer not to, see if your fishmonger is willing to do it for you. Individually stuffing each squid takes a little bit of work, but I can guarantee that the end result will be worth all the extra effort!

FILLING

½ lb (225 g) ground pork

¼ c (45 g) bell peppers, finely chopped

¼ c (45 g) carrots, finely chopped

2 tbsp (30 ml) coconut aminos

½ tsp sea salt

½ tsp black pepper

¼ c (60 g) green onions

1 large egg, room temperature

1 lb (450 g) medium-sized squid, cleaned, heads removed

2 tbsp (30 ml) coconut oil

½ lb (225 g) carrots, sliced

1 small head cauliflower, cut into florets

3 tbsp (10 g) chives, chopped

¼ tsp Aleppo pepper (optional)

DIPPING SAUCE

2 tbsp (30 ml) coconut aminos

1 tbsp (15 ml) lemon juice

1 bird's eye chili pepper

In a cast-iron pan over medium-high heat, add the ground pork. Sauté for 3 to 5 minutes until the pork is no longer pink. Add the bell peppers and carrots, and sauté for 5 minutes. Season with coconut aminos, sea salt and black pepper. Add the green onions and cook for 1 more minute. Turn off the heat and set aside for 10 minutes to cool.

Crack an egg onto the ground pork mixture and mix gently to combine. Spoon the pork filling into each squid leaving a ½-inch (1.5-cm) space toward the opening, and seal each one with a toothpick. This will prevent the filling from spilling out when fried.

Wipe off the same pan and turn on medium heat. Add the coconut oil and stuffed squid. Fry for about 1 to 2 minutes each side. Remove from the pan and set aside. Add the carrots and cauliflower next, and sauté for 5 to 8 minutes until the vegetables are soft. Carefully slice each squid into ½-inch (1.5-cm) rings, top with chopped chives and Aleppo pepper. Serve with sautéed vegetables and dipping sauce on the side.

To prepare the dipping sauce, combine the coconut aminos, lemon juice and bird's eye chili pepper in a small bowl.

chapter two

COMFORTING CASSEROLES

Casseroles can be tough to make when eating Paleo because dairy, pasta and grains are the main components. Gone are the days when I can make a hodgepodge meal by plopping canned ingredients and seasonings from mysterious boxes into a baking dish that will eventually turn into a melted pile of ooey gooey goodness.

Nowadays, I've changed my view on how I look at casseroles. I have embraced the idea that there are recipes that come together and cook in the oven, and there are also those that are cooked stove top but still emulate the richness of a baked casserole such as my No Clay Pot Chicken (page 58). I also consider quiches, like my Breakfast Pizza Quiche (page 69), as casseroles since they are a comforting breakfast staple.

No Clay Pot Chicken

SERVES
4

Clay pot dishes containing salted fish or chicken simmered in dark soy sauce were my entrée selections when we used to eat out at Chinese restaurants. For this healthier version of chicken and rice, you don't need an actual clay pot. A Dutch oven pan or any deep pot will do. Marinated chicken infuses the rice as it slowly steams, and fresh shiitake adds a robust and earthy flavor. The drizzling sauce mimics the sweetness and saltiness of the original clay pot dish sans the soy and preservatives.

1 lb (450 g) boneless, skinless chicken thighs, cut into bite-sized pieces

2 c (400 g) uncooked white rice, rinsed

2 c (450 ml) cold water

3 oz (85 g) fresh shiitake mushrooms, hard stems removed and sliced

1 bunch spinach

¼ c (10 g) green onions, chopped

CHICKEN MARINADE

2 tsp (10 g) fresh ginger, grated

2 tsp (10 g) fresh garlic, minced

¼ c (60 ml) coconut aminos

1 tbsp (15 ml) sesame oil

½ tsp sea salt

2 tbsp (20 g) arrowroot powder

DRIZZLING SAUCE

3 tbsp (45 ml) coconut aminos

1 tbsp (15 ml) raw honey

1 tsp sesame oil

1 tsp chili paste

In a large bowl, place the chicken and the marinade ingredients together. Mix well so that all pieces of the chicken are coated with the marinade. Cover and set aside in the fridge for 30 minutes.

In a Dutch oven pan, add the uncooked white rice and cold water. Cover and turn on the stove to medium heat and cook the rice for 10 minutes. After 10 minutes, the rice will be partially cooked. Stir in half of the shiitake mushrooms with the rice and add the chicken and marinade on top of the rice. Add the rest of the mushrooms. Cover, reduce the heat to low and cook for 12 to 15 minutes.

Once the chicken is cooked, add the spinach and green onions. Mix everything together with the rice. Combine the drizzling sauce and pour it on top. Cover and cook for an additional 5 minutes. Top with more chopped green onions and serve hot.

note: For more detailed instructions on how to rinse uncooked rice, check out the Stove Top Rice recipe on (page 188).

Balsamic Sausage and Vegetables

SERVES
4

Putting together a dish that does not require any additional sautéing is a necessity when I've had a really busy day. Blending basil and oregano with some extra virgin olive oil and balsamic vinegar creates a classic Italian flavor that makes anything and everything taste good. Sausages and any vegetables that need to be cleaned out of my fridge become a one-pot casserole weeknight staple!

2 tbsp (30 ml) balsamic vinegar

2 tbsp (30 ml) extra virgin olive oil

½ tsp dried basil, crushed

½ tsp dried oregano, crushed

½ tsp black pepper

½ tsp sea salt

4 links (340 g) cooked sweet Italian sausages, cut into 1" (2.5 cm) thick slices

1 lb (450 g) cherry tomatoes

1 lb (450 g) yellow sweet potatoes, peeled and cubed into 1" (2.5 cm) pieces

1 large onion, cut into 1" (2.5 cm) pieces

3 tbsp (10 g) chives, chopped

Preheat the oven to 375°F (190°C).

Combine the balsamic vinegar, extra virgin olive oil, basil, oregano, black pepper and sea salt in a small bowl. Whisk to combine.

In a 9 x 13-inch (23 x 33-cm) baking dish, combine the sausages, tomatoes, sweet potatoes and onions. Drizzle in the balsamic seasoning and mix everything together to make sure it coats the sausages and vegetables. Cover with foil and bake for 35 minutes.

Remove from the oven and stir to prevent the bottom from burning. Return to the oven uncovered to bake for another 15 minutes.

Top with chives and let it cool for 5 minutes before serving.

Chicken and Eggplant Parmigiana

I like chicken parmigiana at Italian restaurants, but sometimes I find the breading unnecessary. This is the easiest parmigiana recipe you will find because it's bread-free. In fact, it doesn't have any coating at all, aside from a generous sprinkling of savory spices. Panfrying flattened chicken pieces locks in their juices, and browning the eggplant makes the parmigiana bake superfast. The end result is moist chicken and softened eggplant bathed in rich tomato goodness from the sauce. Totally satisfying!

4 (4 oz [115 g]) boneless, skinless chicken thighs, pounded to ½" (1.3 cm) thickness

1 medium (225 g) eggplant, sliced into ½" (1.3 cm) thick pieces

Garlic powder

Sea salt

Black pepper

2 tbsp (30 ml) ghee

2 c (450 ml) Marinara Sauce (page 189)

½ tsp dried oregano

Preheat the oven to 350°F (180°C).

Generously season the chicken and eggplant slices with garlic powder, sea salt and black pepper. Add ghee to a braiser or Dutch oven pan over medium-high heat. Fry the chicken until lightly browned, about 2 minutes per side. Remove and set aside. Fry the eggplant slices next, 1 minute per side.

Turn off the heat and arrange the eggplant in 2 layers. Add 1 cup (225 ml) of the marinara sauce, spread it evenly on top of the eggplant and sprinkle in half the oregano. Return the chicken pieces to the pan and add the last cup (225 ml) of marinara sauce and sprinkle the remaining oregano.

Cover and place the pan in the oven to bake for 20 to 25 minutes.

Plantain Chilaquiles

SERVES
3

My hairstylist, Angie, planted this idea in my head about making a Paleo version of chilaquiles. We always talk about food whenever she cuts and colors my hair, and we end up feeling hungry all the time! Crushed plantain chips make a great substitute for regular tortilla chips in chilaquiles due to their similar crunchy texture and taste. This is also another way to use up leftover chicken from a previous meal. The eggs act as a binder to hold everything together, and a 50:50 ratio of 2 types of salsa provides a balance of heat and zest. It's the ultimate breakfast food that is crispy, savory and bursting with flavor.

¾ lb (340 g) plantain chips, crushed

½ c (120 ml) mild red salsa

½ c (120 ml) tomatillo salsa

8 oz (225 g) cooked boneless, skinless chicken, shredded

2 large eggs, beaten

1 avocado, chopped

¼ c (10 g) cilantro, chopped

¼ c (10 g) chives, chopped

Extra salsa to serve on the side

Preheat the oven to 375°F (190°C).

Combine the plantain chips, mild red salsa, tomatillo salsa, chicken and eggs in an 8 x 8-inch (20 x 20-cm) baking dish. Mix well. Even out the top with the back of a spoon and bake uncovered for 30 minutes until bubbly around the edges.

Let it rest for 8 minutes. Top with avocado, cilantro and chives. Serve with extra salsa on the side.

Buttered Leek Quiche

SERVES
3

Leeks are milder and sweeter than their onion cousin, and they pair really well with eggs and butter without overpowering them. The thinly sliced pieces soften easily and almost dissolve into the eggs, creating a distinctly creamy texture. For this recipe, I add shredded potatoes and bake until crispy before adding the eggs. The result? A golden hash brown crust baked into the buttery eggs. Mmmm, sinfully good.

FOR THE CRUST

2 lb (900 g) potatoes, shredded

1 tbsp (15 ml) ghee, melted

½ tsp black pepper

½ tsp sea salt

8 large eggs

¼ c (60 ml) Coconut Milk (page 187)

½ tsp paprika

½ tsp sea salt

½ tsp black pepper

½ tsp garlic powder

½ tsp onion powder

2 leek stalks (white parts only), quartered and thinly sliced

2 tbsp (30 g) cold butter, cut into small cubes

Preheat the oven to 425°F (220°C).

Using a nut milk bag or cheesecloth, squeeze out the excess liquid from the potatoes. Season the potatoes with ghee, black pepper and sea salt.

Arrange and press the potatoes on the bottom of an 8 x 8-inch (20 x 20-cm) baking dish until it's about 1" (2.5 cm) thick. This will reduce in half once the potatoes are cooked, so a thicker layer is necessary. Bake in the oven uncovered for 45 minutes until the top is light brown. Remove from the oven and set aside for 5 minutes.

Reduce the oven temperature to 375°F (190°C).

Crack the eggs into a large bowl. Add the coconut milk, paprika, sea salt, black pepper, garlic powder and onion powder. Whisk until light and frothy. Add the leeks to the egg mixture and stir to combine. Pour the mixture on top of the baked potatoes. Randomly distribute the cubed butter pieces on top. Return the baking dish to the oven and bake uncovered for 25 minutes until the eggs are set. Turn off the heat and leave the quiche in the oven for 5 to 8 minutes. Cool slightly before cutting and serving.

Chicken Pesto Zucchini

SERVES
2

Zucchini has become a popular vegetable to turn into noodles thanks to tools such as the spiralizer and julienne peeler. It may look like a lot before cooking, due to its high water content, but it shrinks in half so don't skimp on the zucchini. Dress it up with sun-dried tomato pesto so fresh and aromatic you'll want to eat it on its own.

BASIL AND SUN-DRIED TOMATO PESTO (YIELDS ¾ C [170 G])

6 oz (170 g) basil leaves

¼ c (30 g) raw pine nuts, toasted

3 tbsp (5 g) sun-dried tomatoes

2 cloves garlic

½ tsp black pepper

¼ tsp sea salt

½ c (120 ml) extra virgin olive oil

1 ½ lb (675 g) zucchini, spiralized

1 tbsp (15 ml) ghee

½ lb (225 g) boneless, skinless chicken breast, sliced into bite-sized pieces

Sea salt

Black pepper

¼ c (60 g) Basil and Sun-Dried Tomato Pesto

Prepare the pesto by combining the basil leaves, pine nuts, sun-dried tomatoes, garlic, black pepper and sea salt in a food processor, and pulse for 15 seconds. Scrape the sides and pulse again for 30 more seconds while slowly drizzling the extra virgin olive oil. Set aside ¼ cup (60 g) and store the rest in a glass container in the fridge.

In a wok over medium heat, add the zucchini and sauté for 2 minutes until soft. Remove from the pan and set aside. Drain the excess liquid from the pan and add ghee. Generously season the chicken pieces with salt and pepper. Fry for 5 minutes.

Return the zucchini to the pan and turn off the heat. Add the pesto and mix well to coat the chicken and zucchini with the sauce. Serve immediately.

Garlic Beef with Wilted Greens

SERVES
4

Most people would shy away from garlic-based dishes for fear of ending up with dreaded garlic breath strong enough to clear a room. But, hey, this dish is nothing like that. Garlicky tender slices of sirloin take on a deep, bold taste as they quickly brown in a hot wok, and the garlic turns into soft, caramelized, flavor-packed tidbits. The addition of greens turns this dish into something scrumptious without having to spend a lot of time in the kitchen.

1 lb (450 g) thinly sliced sirloin

¼ c (60 ml) extra virgin olive oil

8 cloves garlic, minced

1 bunch Swiss chard, cut into 2" (5 cm) pieces

1 bunch spinach

¼ tsp red pepper flakes

2 tbsp (30 ml) coconut aminos

Sea salt

Black pepper

Marinate the sirloin in extra virgin olive oil and garlic for 30 minutes to 1 hour.

In a deep skillet or wok over medium-high heat, add the marinated sirloin and stir-fry for 3 minutes. Add the Swiss chard and spinach. Mix together and season with red pepper flakes, coconut aminos, sea salt and black pepper. Sauté continuously until the vegetables are wilted, about 2 to 3 minutes.

Let it rest for 5 minutes before serving.

Cashew Beef

SERVES
4

I have a weakness for anything crunchy, and whenever the craving hits, Cashew Beef definitely fits the bill. Toasted cashews add a nice crunch and smokiness to ground beef, plus red and green bell peppers give it a colorful hue. I highly recommend using raw cashews and toasting them on a dry wok for better flavor rather than the prepackaged ones that may contain added oil and salt. It also gives you control over how toasted you want the cashews to be.

1 c (115 g) raw whole cashews

2 tsp (10 ml) tallow or coconut oil

1 ½ lb (675 g) ground beef

2 tbsp (20 g) ginger, grated

1 tbsp (10 g) garlic, minced

¼ c (60 ml) coconut aminos

1 green bell pepper, sliced into strips

1 red bell pepper, sliced into strips

1 small onion, sliced

1 (8 oz [225 g]) can water chestnuts, sliced

Sea salt

Black pepper

In a wok over medium heat, add the raw cashews. Toast for a couple of minutes until lightly browned. Stir consistently to prevent the nuts from burning. Remove and set aside.

Add tallow to the same wok. Add the ground beef and stir-fry for 5 minutes until browned. Add the ginger, garlic and coconut aminos. Stir-fry until fragrant. Add the bell peppers, onion and water chestnuts. Cook until the vegetables start to soften but are still crisp, about 5 minutes. Season with sea salt and black pepper.

Turn off the heat and mix in toasted cashews before serving.

Pork and Green Beans

SERVES
4

Butternut squash is a good source of starchy carbohydrates, fiber and vitamin A. Enjoy it in abundance during fall and winter when it's widely available and locally sourced. Reap the benefits of butternut squash with this no-fuss meat-and-vegetable sauté that is sweet, savory and hearty. Leftovers are great for breakfast with a fried egg on top!

1 lb (450 g) ground pork

4 cloves garlic, minced

1 small onion, sliced

1 beefsteak tomato, sliced

¼ c (60 ml) coconut aminos

1 tsp fish sauce

Black pepper

1 lb (450 g) butternut squash, cubed

1 lb (450 g) green beans

Sea salt

Add the pork to a deep skillet or wok over medium-high heat. Sauté for 5 to 6 minutes until it is cooked and no longer pink. Add the garlic and onions. Sauté for 1 minute.

Add the tomato slices, and cook for 5 minutes until they are soft. Gently press the tomato slices to extract their juices. Season with the coconut aminos, fish sauce and black pepper.

Reduce the heat to medium-low and add the butternut squash. Mix, cover and cook for 10 minutes. Check at the halfway mark to make sure the bottom doesn't burn. Give the pork and butternut squash a quick sauté. Add the green beans and mix. Cover and cook for another 10 minutes. Season with sea salt and black pepper to taste.

Remove the cover and sauté everything for 3 more minutes before serving.

Sweet-and-Sour Pork

SERVES
4

In a world of convenience, we see recipes that make use of little packets of sauce mix. These require very little preparation and turn into a quick meal for the entire family. Pork bits coated in flour, deep-fried in vats of oil and then coated with these sauce packets may just be one of the unhealthiest foods out there. No need to settle for that! There is no gluten breading in this recipe, but you won't be left hanging. A light dredging of tapioca and coconut flour gives this dish an airy texture and absorbs the sweet-and-sour sauce. With the right balance of sweetness and tanginess from the pineapple, you'll be coming back for more.

PORK MARINADE

¼ c (60 ml) coconut aminos

2 tbsp (30 ml) rice vinegar

2 cloves garlic, minced

1 lb (450 g) thin pork chops, cut into bite-sized pieces

Black pepper

Sea salt

¼ c (30 g) tapioca flour

2 tbsp (15 g) coconut flour

1 c (225 ml) tallow or coconut oil

½ head cauliflower, cut into florets

1 bell pepper, sliced

1 large carrot, sliced

1 (20 oz [570 g]) can pineapple chunks, drained, 1 c (225 ml) of juice set aside

2 cloves garlic, minced

2 tbsp (30 ml) apple cider vinegar

4 tbsp (60 ml) coconut aminos

1 tsp tapioca flour dissolved in 2 tbsp (30 ml) warm water

Combine the pork marinade ingredients in a bowl, add the pork and marinate for 1 hour.

Remove the pork pieces from the marinade, pat dry and season with black pepper and sea salt. Combine the tapioca and coconut flour in a bowl. Lightly dredge each piece of pork in the flour mixture and shake off the excess.

Heat tallow in a wok on medium-high heat. Add the pork and fry in 2 batches to avoid overcrowding. Once golden brown, after 4 to 5 minutes, remove and set aside on a serving plate.

Drain the excess oil from the wok, leaving about 1 tablespoon (15 ml) for stir-frying. Add the cauliflower, bell pepper, carrot and pineapple chunks. Stir-fry for 3 to 4 minutes. Add the garlic and stir-fry until fragrant, about 1 minute. Reduce the heat to low and add the pineapple juice, apple cider vinegar and coconut aminos. Let it simmer for 8 minutes. Pour in the dissolved tapioca and stir until the sauce begins to thicken. Turn off the heat and return the fried pork pieces to the pan. Mix together until covered with the sauce. Serve immediately.

Sweet Pepper Shrimp Sauté

SERVES
4

There is no better way to showcase the flavor of fresh shrimp than to lightly complement it with the sweetness of bell peppers and the zest of lemon. This quick-and-easy dish takes less than half an hour to prepare and cook, making it perfect for a weeknight meal.

2 tbsp (30 ml) tallow or coconut oil

2 lb (900 g) raw jumbo shrimp, shell on, deveined

1 yellow bell pepper, sliced into 3" (7.7 cm) strips

1 red bell pepper, sliced into 3" (7.7 cm) strips

2 c (260 g) sweet onions, sliced

1 tsp dried thyme, crushed

¼ tsp sea salt

½ tsp black pepper

Juice and zest of 2 lemons

3 tbsp (10 g) fresh flat-leaf parsley, roughly chopped

In a wok on medium-high heat, add 1 tablespoon (15 ml) of tallow. Add the shrimp and stir-fry until they turn pink, about 2 to 3 minutes. Remove the cooked shrimp from the wok and set aside in a bowl.

Add the last tablespoon (15 ml) of tallow to the wok, and then add the yellow and red bell peppers, onions, thyme, sea salt and black pepper. Sauté until the onions become translucent, about 4 to 5 minutes.

Add the cooked shrimp back to the wok and mix them with the onions and peppers. Reduce the heat to medium and let them cook for 2 to 3 more minutes.

Remove from the heat, drizzle with fresh lemon juice and top with lemon zest and chopped parsley.

Balsamic Sardines

SERVES
2

I like eating sardines straight from the can as a snack, and when I want to enjoy this as a quick meal, I whip up this balsamic sauté in no time. If you haven't braved canned sardines before, season them with balsamic vinegar to make it easier on the palate.

1 ½ lb (675 g) zucchini, spiralized

1 tsp ghee

½ lb (225 g) cherry tomatoes, cut in half

2 (4.30 oz [125 g]) cans sardines, oil or water drained

1 tbsp (15 ml) balsamic vinegar

¼ tsp sea salt

2 tbsp (10 g) parsley, chopped

In a deep skillet or wok over medium-high heat, add the zucchini and sauté for 2 minutes until it starts to soften. Remove and set aside. Drain the excess liquid from the pan and add ghee.

Add the cherry tomatoes to the pan and sauté for 2 minutes. Add the sardines and balsamic vinegar. Season with sea salt. Return the zucchini noodles to the pan and cook for another 2 minutes.

Sprinkle the chopped parsley on top before serving.

Brussels Sprouts Favorite

SERVES
4

This is a versatile one-pot meal that I make when I'm in a pinch for time. I use vegetables depending on what's in season, so feel free to make your own version once you've tried this base recipe. It's easy and packed with flavor, and I'm sure it will become one of your favorite meals as well!

1 tbsp (15 ml) ghee or coconut oil

1 medium sweet onion, cubed

1 c (55 g) sun-dried tomatoes, sliced into strips

1 lb (450 g) grass-fed beef hotdogs, sliced into ½" (1.5 cm) pieces

1 lb (450 g) Brussels sprouts, medium-sized, cut into halves

½ lb (225 g) sweet potatoes, cubed

¼ c (60 ml) water

Juice and zest of 1 lemon

3 cloves garlic, minced

½ tsp black pepper

¼ c (60 ml) hot cayenne sauce

Add ghee to a wok or skillet over medium-high heat. Add the onions and sun-dried tomatoes. Sauté until the onions are soft, about 3 minutes. Add the hotdogs and cook for 5 minutes until lightly browned. Remove the onions, sun-dried tomatoes and hotdogs from the pan and set aside in a bowl.

Add the Brussels sprouts and sweet potatoes to the wok. Lower the heat to medium-low and add water. Cover and simmer until the sprouts turn bright green and the sweet potatoes can easily be pierced by a fork, about 10 to 12 minutes. If the water has completely evaporated before the sprouts and sweet potatoes are cooked, add another ¼ cup (60 ml) of water.

Return the hotdog mixture to the wok and season with lemon juice, lemon zest, garlic, black pepper and hot sauce. Mix everything together and cook for 3 more minutes until all the flavors are incorporated.

Moorish Skewers

SERVES
4

At the Barrio Santa Cruz tapas bar in Seville, skewered meat, or *pinchitos morunos*, is popular local fare that has Moorish origins. Cubed meat, typically beef, is marinated overnight in a blend of more than 10 spices, then grilled to perfection. I took the guesswork out of the spice combination and came up with one that tastes just like the one we had in Seville! Take note that these are small servings, which is what tapas is usually about, so it's ideal as a light meal or heavy snack.

MARINATED BEETS

4 cooked beets, sliced

2 tbsp (30 ml) red wine vinegar

2 tbsp (30 ml) extra virgin olive oil

2 cloves garlic, minced

Sea salt

SPICE SEASONING

½ tsp sea salt

1 ½ tsp (10 g) dried oregano, crushed

¾ tsp turmeric powder

1 tsp cumin

¼ tsp black pepper

1 piece star anise, ground

½ tsp garlic powder

⅛ tsp cayenne pepper

⅛ tsp nutmeg

⅛ tsp paprika

2 tbsp (30 ml) extra virgin olive oil

1 tbsp (15 ml) apple cider vinegar

1 lb (450 g) beef sirloin, cut into
1 ½" (4 cm) pieces

½ lb (225 g) pearl onions

½ lb (225 g) button mushrooms

½ lb (225 g) carrots, sliced into
½" (1.3 cm) pieces

2 tsp (10 ml) coconut oil

In a small zip-top bag, combine all the ingredients for the Marinated Beets. Seal and let it marinate for an hour in the fridge.

Combine all the ingredients for the spice seasoning in a gallon-sized (3.75 L) zip-top plastic bag. Add the extra virgin olive oil and apple cider vinegar. Shake to combine. Add the cubed beef to the marinade, press out the excess air and seal. Lightly massage the bag to make sure the marinade coats every piece of beef. Place it in the fridge to marinate for an hour.

Thread the beef on wooden skewers and set aside. Skewer the pearl onions, mushrooms and carrots, and set aside with the beef.

Preheat the grill for 10 minutes on high, then reduce the heat to medium. Lightly brush grates with 1 teaspoon of coconut oil.

Place the beef skewers on the grill and cook for 8 to 10 minutes, turning each skewer every 2 minutes to avoid burning and overcooking one side. Once cooked, remove from the heat and set aside to rest for 5 minutes.

Baste the vegetable skewers with the remaining coconut oil. Place on the grill, flipping every couple of minutes until cooked and lightly charred. Serve together with the beef skewers and Marinated Beets.

note: Cooked beets vacuum-sealed and ready to use can be found in any grocery store. Another side alternative to the grilled onions, mushrooms and carrots is alternating pitted green olives, roasted red peppers and pepperoncini on bamboo skewers and serving them cold.

Charcoal Grilled Skewers (*Yakitori*)

SERVES 4

Yakitori is fun, interactive and best enjoyed outdoors, especially during grilling season. We have a terracotta tabletop charcoal grill shaped like a pig that is a permanent fixture on our picnic table, and we use it specifically for *yakitori*. Using a charcoal grill may seem old school, but it imparts a smoky flavor that's hard to replicate using a regular gas grill. Basting each skewer a couple times while grilling and one last time before serving creates a lip-smacking sweet-and-savory finish.

1 lb (450 g) boneless, skinless chicken thighs, cut into 2" (5 cm) pieces

5 stalks green onions, cut into 2" (5 cm) pieces

Sea salt

1 lb (450 g) skinless salmon, cut into 2" (5 cm) pieces

¼ lb (115 g) grape tomatoes

3 oz (85 g) shiitake mushrooms, wiped clean and stems removed

¾ lb (340 g) asparagus, hard ends trimmed off and cut into 2" (5 cm) pieces

½ lb (225 g) smoked bacon strips, cut into 3 equal pieces

BASTING SAUCE

¾ c (180 ml) coconut aminos

¼ c (60 ml) raw honey

2 cloves garlic, minced

2 tbsp (20 g) shallots, chopped

1 tsp ginger, grated

¼ tsp red pepper flakes

1 tsp coconut oil

Beginning with the chicken and green onions, hold a piece of green onion perpendicular to the skewer and pierce it through the middle. Alternate it with a strip of chicken skewered lengthwise. Work this way until the skewer is full with about 4 to 5 pieces of chicken and green onions. Season with sea salt and set aside.

Next, alternately skewer the salmon with the green onions. Season with sea salt and set aside.

Skewer the grape tomatoes and shiitake mushrooms. Pierce both from the side so that they won't fall off during grilling. Set aside.

Wrap each piece of asparagus with a piece of bacon. Skewer it perpendicularly and pierce through the edge of the bacon flap to secure it.

Use a chimney starter to prepare the charcoal for the grill. While this is heating up, prepare the basting sauce. Combine the coconut aminos, honey, garlic, shallots, ginger and red pepper flakes in a deep bowl. Using a handheld immersion blender, puree the sauce until smooth.

When the grill is ready, brush some coconut oil on the grate to prevent the meat from sticking. Grill the chicken and salmon skewers for 2 to 3 minutes on the first side. Flip and then baste it with the sauce. Cook for 1 minute. Flip and baste again. The skewers are cooked once they are lightly charred, the chicken pieces are no longer pink and the salmon is firm. Grill the vegetables for 1 to 2 minutes on each side and baste with the sauce after flipping.

Baste all the skewers with some more sauce and let them cool for a couple of minutes before eating.

note: No charcoal grill? This can also be cooked on a gas or electric grill. The cooking times should roughly be the same.

Honey Dijon Salmon Steaks

SERVES
2

I could eat salmon every day, but I prefer simple seasonings that are not overpowering. Honey with Dijon mustard is a sweet tease that delivers a sharp and spicy kick, so a little bit goes a long way! Slather it on top of each salmon steak for an easy meal that looks so fancy you'll feel like a gourmet chef.

1 tsp ghee, melted

1 lb (450 g) sweet potatoes, skin on and cubed

1 ½ tbsp (20 g) whole Dijon mustard

Zest of 1 lemon

¼ tsp sea salt

¼ tsp black pepper

1 tbsp (15 ml) raw honey

1 tsp lemon juice

2 (4 oz [115 g]) salmon steaks, about ¾" (2 cm) thick

Preheat the oven to 425°F (220°C) and line a rimmed baking sheet with parchment paper.

Toss the sweet potatoes with melted ghee, ½ tablespoon (10 g) of whole Dijon mustard, lemon zest, salt and pepper. Arrange them evenly on the baking sheet and cook for 8 minutes.

Meanwhile, rinse the salmon and pat dry with paper towels. Combine the remaining 1 tablespoon (15 g) of whole Dijon mustard with raw honey and lemon juice in a small bowl.

Once the sweet potatoes are partially cooked, remove the baking sheet from the oven and flip them to cook on the other side. Push them to one end of the baking sheet and place the salmon steaks next to them. Generously coat each piece of salmon with the honey mustard seasoning. Bake for 15 minutes or until the salmon flakes easily with a fork and the sweet potatoes are cooked through.

Blackened Trout
with Mango Papaya Salsa

SERVES
4

Trout fillets are great because they do not have as many bones as whole trout. In this recipe, they take on a Southern flair when coated with a bold and sassy blackening seasoning that will make you say, "Hey y'all!" Generously top them with a Mango Papaya Salsa for that extra special touch.

MANGO PAPAYA SALSA

2 c (330 g) ripe mango, chopped

2 c (330 g) ripe papaya, chopped

1 jalapeño, seeds and stem removed, chopped

1 medium cucumber, chopped

1 small red onion, chopped

Juice of 1 lime

Sea salt

1 lb (450 g) trout fillet, skin on

1 tbsp (15 ml) ghee, melted

BLACKENING SEASONING

½ tsp cayenne pepper

½ tsp black pepper

½ tsp sea salt

2 tsp (10 g) paprika

½ tsp onion powder

½ tsp garlic powder

½ tsp cumin

½ tsp dried oregano, crushed

½ tsp dried thyme

¼ tsp dried sage

Preheat the oven to 350°F (180°C).

Prepare the salsa by combining mango, papaya, jalapeño, cucumber, red onion and lime juice in a bowl. Season with sea salt, cover and refrigerate to chill.

Lightly coat both sides of the trout fillets with ghee and place them skin side down on a baking sheet. Combine the blackening seasoning ingredients in a small bowl. Generously season each fillet, pressing gently so that it evenly covers every exposed surface.

Bake in the oven for 12 to 15 minutes. Let them cool for 5 minutes before topping with the Mango Papaya Salsa.

Crab and Shrimp-Topped Salmon

SERVES 4

Ready-made stuffed salmon may seem convenient, but they are filled with a paragraph-long list of questionable ingredients that make my head spin. The topping in this recipe is chock full of plump crabmeat and shrimp with a little bit of onion, mayo and spices. That alone makes it restaurant worthy! For fresh fish and seafood, there's no need for unnecessary add-ons other than a squeeze of lemon juice for that extra zing.

¼ lb (115 g) lump crab meat

¼ lb (115 g) raw shrimp, chopped

¼ c (10 g) onion, minced

6 tbsp (90 g) Mayonnaise (page 187)

1 tsp paprika

Sea salt

Black pepper

4 (6 oz [170 g]) wild salmon fillets, skin on

1 tbsp (15 ml) ghee, melted

1 ½ lb (675 g) asparagus, woody ends trimmed off

Lemon wedges

Preheat the oven to 375°F (190°C) and line a rimmed baking sheet with parchment paper.

Prepare the topping by combining the crab meat, shrimp, onion, mayonnaise and paprika in a bowl.

Season the salmon fillets with sea salt and black pepper. Place the fillets next to each other on one side of the baking sheet. Top each one with equal amounts of the crab mixture. These are generous portions so don't worry if the topping overflows!

Coat the asparagus with ghee and place them next to the fish. Bake in the oven for 20 to 25 minutes until the salmon flakes easily with a fork. Switch to broil and cook for an additional 2 minutes until the topping is lightly browned. Serve with lemon wedges on the side.

Shrimp-Stuffed Baked Sweet Potato

SERVES 4

Inspired by a quaint café tucked in a corner at Disneyland that offers shrimp salad on a gigantic baked potato, this recipe features sweet potatoes loaded with a big helping of shrimp. Combining the fleshy pulp of the sweet potato with mayonnaise, paprika and seafood seasoning produces a creamy stuffing that's made even creamier when topped with avocado.

4 large sweet potatoes

2 tbsp (30 ml) ghee, melted

1 lb (450 g) cooked medium shrimp, shells removed

¼ c (60 g) Mayonnaise (page 187)

¼ tsp paprika

¼ tsp seafood seasoning, I like Old Bay

2 tsp (10 ml) lemon juice

⅛ tsp sea salt

1 avocado, chopped

2 tbsp (10 g) chives, chopped

Preheat the oven to 375°F (190°C).

Lightly coat the sweet potatoes with 1 tablespoon (15 ml) of ghee and place them on a baking sheet. Bake for 45 minutes. Cut them in half and coat with the remaining 1 tablespoon (15 ml) of ghee. Return to the oven and bake for 30 more minutes.

Once cooked, scoop the middle portion of the sweet potatoes into a bowl and leave ¼" (1.3 mm) in the shells. Mash the sweet potato pulp. Add the cooked shrimp, mayonnaise, paprika, seafood seasoning, lemon juice and sea salt. Gently mix until combined and fill each sweet potato half shell with the mixture.

Top with chopped avocados and chives, and serve immediately.

Chunky Chili

I don't know about you, but to me, bite-sized chunks of beef taste so much better than ground meat in chili. I like to be able to chew it, rather than just swirl it in my mouth and gulp it down! This has a bit of heat with just a smidge of cayenne, so it's not really spicy at all. Fire-roasted instead of regular tomatoes give it a smokiness that is fantastic with the beef. Topped with onions, avocados and plantains, each spoonful is guaranteed to be a delight.

1 tbsp (15 ml) tallow or bacon fat

1 lb (450 g) beef chuck, cut into ½" (1.5 cm) cubes

½ c (65 g) onion, sliced

½ c (25 g) carrots, sliced

3 cloves garlic, minced

2 tbsp (30 g) tomato paste

½ tsp cayenne pepper

1 tbsp (15 g) chili powder

1 tbsp (15 g) cumin

½ tsp dried oregano, crushed

Sea salt

Black pepper

1 (14.5 oz [410 g]) can diced fire-roasted tomatoes

½ c (120 ml) Beef Bone Broth (page 185)

TOPPINGS

¼ c (40 g) onion, chopped

1 medium avocado, chopped

¼ c (40 g) plantain chips, crushed

In a Dutch oven pan over medium heat, add the tallow and beef. Brown for 3 to 4 minutes. Add the onions, carrots and garlic and sauté for 5 minutes until onions are translucent. Add the tomato paste, cayenne pepper, chili powder, cumin, oregano, sea salt and black pepper. Stir together and cook for 1 minute. Add the diced tomatoes and broth and reduce the heat to low. Cover and simmer for 2 hours stirring occasionally.

Spoon into bowls and serve with onions, avocados and plantain chips on top.

Easy Cioppino

SERVES 4

Cioppino always brings me back to San Francisco and this one restaurant at Fisherman's Wharf. Since I have access to fresh and affordable seafood all year-round, homemade cioppino is relatively easy to make. The soup base takes a little bit of time to prepare, but once it's ready, it doesn't take long to cook the fish and seafood, so I'm always ready on the side with my big soup bowl!

1 tbsp (15 ml) ghee

1 c (130 g) onion, sliced

3 cloves garlic, minced

1 c (225 ml) dry white wine

1 tbsp (15 g) dried parsley

1 tsp dried oregano

Pinch of red pepper flakes (optional)

2 c (450 ml) Vegetable Broth
(page 186)

3 ½ c (875 ml) Marinara Sauce
(page 189)

2 lb (900 g) black mussels

1 lb (450 g) crab legs

½ lb (225 g) halibut fish
(or any white fish)

1 bunch Swiss chard, chopped

5 sprigs fresh parsley, chopped

Melt ghee in a Dutch oven pan or stockpot over medium heat. Add the onions and garlic. Sauté until fragrant, about 2 minutes. Add the white wine and simmer until reduced by half. Season with dried parsley, oregano and red pepper flakes. Add the vegetable broth and marinara sauce. Stir and bring to a boil. Reduce the heat to low and simmer for 1 ½ hours, stirring occasionally.

Add the mussels, crab legs and fish. Cook for 5 to 8 minutes. Remove the unopened mussel shells and add Swiss chard. Turn off the heat, cover and let it sit for 2 minutes until the Swiss chard is wilted. Top with fresh parsley and serve.

Peruvian Chicken Lime Soup (*Aguadito de Pollo*)

SERVES
4

My first taste of Peruvian food was at this place in Gardena that my husband took me to years ago. It's a small chain that serves great Peruvian food, and I'm thrilled to finally be able to create my own version of its *Aguadito de Pollo*. I gave it some pizazz by loading it up with tidbits of colorful vegetables, such as green beans, carrots and potatoes. Amidst its bone broth goodness, the cilantro and lime shine through, giving it a refreshing taste that will definitely make you crave more. I burned my tongue a couple of times when I made this because I couldn't wait for it to cool down!

1 bunch cilantro

½ c (120 ml) water

3 cloves garlic

1 tbsp (15 ml) tallow or coconut oil

1 lb (450 g) boneless, skinless chicken thighs, chopped into ½" (1.5 cm) cubes

Sea salt

1 medium onion, chopped

½ tsp fish sauce

5 c (1.25 L) Chicken Bone Broth (page 185)

¼ lb (115 g) green beans, chopped into ½" (1.5 cm) pieces

¼ lb (115 g) carrots, chopped into ¼" (6 mm) cubes

¼ lb (115 g) potatoes, chopped into ¼" (6 mm) cubes

2 tbsp (25 g) uncooked white rice

2 tbsp (30 ml) lime juice

Lime wedges for serving

Place the cilantro, water and garlic in a blender. Pulse until it is a pasty consistency.

Add tallow to a Dutch oven pan over medium heat. Generously season the chicken with sea salt and brown for 8 minutes, stirring occasionally. Add the cilantro puree, onions and fish sauce. Mix and let it cook for 5 minutes. Add the bone broth and bring to a boil.

Reduce the heat to low. Cover and simmer for 35 minutes. Add the green beans, carrots, potatoes and rice. Cover and simmer for 15 more minutes. Add the lime juice before serving and serve with lime wedges.

Glass Noodle Soup (*Sotanghon*)

Sotanghon reminds me of rainy days when I was growing up. My mom would make this, and its wonderful aroma would fill our house. Swapping regular glass noodles for ones made with kelp makes this a good choice if you are looking for a low-carb meal. Slurp this soup with gusto and don't be shy to go for that extra helping!

2 tbsp (30 ml) tallow or coconut oil

½ lb (225 g) boneless, skinless chicken thighs, cubed

Sea salt

5 cloves garlic, minced

½ c (75 g) onion, chopped

3 oz (85 g) shiitake mushrooms, sliced

½ c (25 g) carrot, julienned

1 dozen medium shrimp, peeled and cut in half

3 c (675 ml) Chicken Bone Broth (page 185)

2 c (450 ml) water

12 oz (340 g) kelp noodles

½ tsp fish sauce

½ tsp paprika

Black pepper

¼ c (10 g) green onions, chopped

Add tallow to a Dutch oven pan over medium heat. Generously season the chicken with sea salt. Fry for 2 minutes. Add the garlic, onions and shiitake mushrooms. Stir-fry until fragrant, about 3 minutes. Add the carrots and shrimp. Cook for another 3 minutes. Add the chicken bone broth, water and kelp noodles. Bring to a boil. Season with fish sauce, paprika and black pepper. Adjust the sea salt if necessary. Cover and reduce the heat to low. Let it simmer for 10 minutes until the kelp noodles soften.

Top with green onions before serving.

Seafood Coconut Stew (*Ginataan*)

SERVES
4

During Thanksgiving and Christmas at our relative's house, one of our aunties brings a gigantic pot of Seafood Coconut Stew. The lucky ones who are there on time get first dibs on the prime pieces. Cooking with coconut milk enhances the flavor of seafood and gives it a wonderful finish. For the chili lovers out there, add a little bit of red pepper flakes for that extra kick.

1 tbsp (15 ml) coconut oil

1 ½ c (195 g) onion, sliced

2" (5 cm) ginger, sliced

2 lb (900 g) blue crabs, cut in half

1 lb (450 g) littleneck clams

1 lb (450 g) medium-sized shrimp, heads on

2 c (450 ml) Coconut Milk (page 187)

1 lb (450 g) butternut squash, cubed into 1" (2.5 cm) pieces

1 bunch spinach

4 stalks green onions, sliced into 2" (5 cm) pieces

Add coconut oil to a large Dutch oven pan on medium-high heat. Add the onions and ginger. Sauté for 3 minutes. Add the crabs, clams and shrimp. Cover and cook for 5 minutes. Stir in the coconut milk. Once it simmers, add the butternut squash. Cover and reduce the heat to medium-low. Let it cook for 20 minutes, stirring halfway so that it cooks evenly. Check if the butternut squash is cooked by piercing it with a fork. Cook for 5 to 8 more minutes if needed. Add the spinach and green onions. Stir and simmer for 3 minutes. Serve immediately.

Chicken and Rice Porridge (*Arroz Caldo*)

SERVES
4

When I feel like I'm coming down with something, I make this thick and comforting porridge to make me feel better. It is similar to Chinese congee but the ginger and fish sauce make this uniquely Filipino. Load it up with any toppings you like for the ultimate comfort food!

1 tbsp (15 ml) ghee or coconut oil

6 cloves garlic, minced

1 c (150 g) shallots, chopped

3" (7.5 cm) ginger, grated

1 ½ lb (675 g) chicken wing drummettes, skin on

Sea salt

Black pepper

1 tbsp (15 ml) fish sauce

¼ tsp paprika

5 c (1.25 L) water

¾ c (150 g) uncooked white rice

2 tbsp (30 ml) lemon juice

TOPPINGS

4 large hard-boiled eggs, sliced

¼ c (10 g) green onions, chopped

Lemon wedges for serving

Pork cracklings, optional

Add ghee to a Dutch oven pan over medium heat. Add the garlic, shallots and ginger. Sauté for 2 minutes until fragrant.

Generously season the chicken pieces with sea salt and black pepper. Add to the pot and fry for 3 to 4 minutes until the skin is lightly browned. Season with fish sauce and paprika, and sauté. Add water and bring to a boil. Cover the pot and reduce the heat to low. Simmer for 20 minutes. Add the white rice and stir. Cover and cook for 35 minutes, stirring occasionally to make sure the rice doesn't stick to the bottom as it cooks. It is ready once the broth has thickened and the rice is very soft. A little bit of liquid is okay since the rice will continue to absorb it. Stir in the lemon juice and adjust the sea salt and black pepper if desired.

Ladle into serving bowls and top with hard-boiled eggs and green onions, and serve with lemon wedges on the side.

note: If you can find it, pork cracklings make a great topping in addition to the hard-boiled eggs and green onions.

chapter six

SENSATIONAL SALADS

Bright and colorful salads remind me of warm summer days and lazy summer nights. They are wonderful as a light meal or a filling entrée, depending on how much protein is added.

A well-crafted salad exudes freshness and vibrancy, making it such a wonderful treat for the senses. Homemade dressing is the perfect complement and takes only a few minutes to make a fresh batch every time. It tastes so much better and definitely beats the bottled and preservative-laden ones from the grocery stores.

The salads in this section include a fresh take on all-time classics such as Chicken Salad Wraps (page 170) and Antipasto (page 174). If you don't feel like turning on the stove, make a big bowl of salad to savor and enjoy!

Chicken Salad Wraps

SERVES
2

If you have leftover chicken, using it in a chicken salad is the perfect way to repurpose it and create a brand-new meal. People won't even suspect they are eating leftovers when they try this classic with a twist. It is loaded with fruits, vegetables and nuts to turn the ordinary into something extraordinary!

8 oz (225 g) boneless, skinless cooked chicken, chopped

½ c (90 g) red seedless grapes, halved

1 rib celery, chopped

1 small shallot, chopped

3 tbsp (20 g) dried cranberries

3 tbsp (45 g) Mayonnaise (page 187)

3 tbsp (20 g) raw almonds, chopped

⅛ tsp sea salt

¼ tsp black pepper

1 head butter lettuce leaves

In a bowl, add all the ingredients except the butter lettuce and mix thoroughly until well combined. Cover and chill for at least half an hour. Serve with the butter lettuce leaves.

Grilled Romaine

SERVES
2

Grilled salads scream summer. Who knew grilled romaine could taste so good? Red-hot flames caramelize the vegetables and give them a sweet and smoky flavor that goes so well with chicken. Drizzled with a sweet-and-tangy maple lime vinaigrette, this makes for a light and refreshing meal.

2 (4 oz [115 g]) boneless, skin-on chicken thighs

¼ tsp paprika

2 tbsp (30 ml) lime juice

Sea salt

Black pepper

1 tsp coconut oil

2 romaine hearts, cut in half

½ lb (225 g) carrots, tops removed

1 medium red onion, quartered

2 limes cut in half

MAPLE LIME VINAIGRETTE

2 tbsp (30 ml) lime juice

2 tbsp (30 ml) maple syrup

¼ c (60 ml) extra virgin olive oil

Zest of 1 lime

1 tsp whole mustard

1 tbsp (5 g) chives, chopped

In a bowl, combine the chicken with paprika and lime juice. Marinate for 15 minutes.

Preheat the grill on high for 8 minutes and reduce the heat to medium. Remove the chicken from the marinade and season with sea salt and black pepper. Lightly brush grates with coconut oil. Arrange the romaine, carrots, onions and limes on one side. Add the marinated chicken skin side down on the other side.

Grill the vegetables for 5 to 6 minutes, turning occasionally until they start to caramelize. Remove and set aside on a serving plate. Grill the chicken thighs, turning once until the skin is crispy and the meat is no longer pink. The internal temperature should be around 170°F (76°C). Place them on the same serving plate as the vegetables. Let them rest for 5 minutes.

Prepare the maple lime vinaigrette by combining all the vinaigrette ingredients except the chives in a deep bowl or cup. Using an immersion blender, pulse until it becomes smooth and creamy. Mix in the chives and drizzle the vinaigrette on top of the grilled vegetables and chicken. Serve immediately.

Antipasto

I'm a fan of make-ahead salads, especially those that can easily be tossed together, and then chilled overnight in the fridge. When you only have a few minutes and no time to cook, prepare this the night before and you'll have a ready meal the next day. Pop open a bottle of chilled sparkling water and pour it into a tall glass with a slice of lemon to sip while you eat the antipasto for a quaint Italian feel.

1 (14 oz [400 g]) can artichoke hearts, drained and quartered

6 oz (170 g) pitted black olives, drained

3 oz (85 g) sun-dried tomatoes

15 cornichons

6 oz (170 g) uncured pepperoni, quartered

10 pepperoncini

2 tbsp (5 g) flat-leaf parsley, chopped

BALSAMIC RED WINE VINAIGRETTE

1 tbsp (15 ml) balsamic vinegar

1 tbsp (15 ml) red wine vinegar

¼ c (60 ml) extra virgin olive oil

1 tsp whole mustard

1 clove garlic, minced

¼ tsp sea salt

¼ tsp black pepper

In a large bowl, combine the artichoke hearts, olives, sun-dried tomatoes, cornichons, pepperoni, pepperoncini and parsley.

Prepare the balsamic red wine vinaigrette by combining all the vinaigrette ingredients in a deep bowl or cup. Using an immersion blender, pulse until the vinaigrette becomes smooth and creamy. Drizzle the balsamic red wine vinaigrette on top of the antipasto and mix to combine. Chill in the fridge for 30 minutes before serving.

Index